Revival, Enlightenment, and Awakening

The Divine Intelligence of Eternity in Fire and Water

Joseph Kahuho Gatoto

Revival, Enlightenment, and Awakening   Joseph Kahuho Gatoto

Revival, Enlightenment, and Awakening

The Divine Intelligences of Eternity in Fire and Water

Author Contacts

Phone +254715656938 (WhatsApp and Calls)

Email: intergratedlifeministry@gmail.com

Facebook: Kahuho Gatoto

YouTube: Kahuho Gatoto

Feel free to contact me for questions, comments, seminars, and other ministry invitations.

Books in the ongoing Reality Series

1. The Pneumatic Nature of Reality

2. Metaverse: The Metaphysical Nature of Life

3. Reverberation

4. Energy

5. Reality and Probability

6. Humanity: The Framework of Human Existence Volume 1

7. Reality of Music

8. A History of Time

9. Consciousness: The Framework of Human Existence

10. Incongruent Congruent: Poems of Formation

11. Higher Realities of Human Existence

12. Concepts from Existence and Three Lectures from Scribble

13. Ancient Realities: Into the Ancient One

14. His Image and Likeness: Sons

15. Quantum Reality and Quantum Entanglement: Harmonic Convergence

16. Oneness: The Reality of Reality

17. Eternity and The Four Living Letters: The Age of Trinity and The Realities Thereof

18. The Groom and His Bride: Contemplations on Christ, The Church, and Marriage

19. Principles of Reality

20. Telepathy, Telepathic Unity, Precognition, and Postcognition

21. Quantum Re-creation and Healing

22. Ecstasy: The Truth Concerning Pleasure and Happiness

23. Love: The One True Light - The Highest Intelligence and Highest Consciousness

24. Memory - The Power of Recall: A Gateway to Ecstasy and Conscious Alteration

25. Ascension and Transcendency

26. Christ: The Life, Essence, Intelligence, and The Perfection of Love

27. Quantum Beings: The Framework of Human Existence Volume 2

28. Water – The Glory of Water

29. Prayer – The Metaphysical and Mystical Realities of Prayer

30. Becoming Divine - Humanity's Destiny

31. Eternity Volume 2

32. The Self That Is I - The Soul and Its Manifold Realities: The Framework of Human Existence Volume 3

33. I AM WE ARE - The Framework of Human Existence Volume 4

34. Self Knowings - The Framework of Human Existence Volume 5

35. Higher Self Implications - The Framework of Humanity Volume 6

36. The Self That Is I - The Soul and Its Manifold Realities Volume 2: The Framework of Humanity Volume 7

37. The Self That Is I - The Soul and Its Manifold Realities Volume 3: The Framework of Humanity Volume 8

38. The Quantum Field and The Sub-Quantum Field – The Subtle Metaphysical Dimension of Earth and the Cosmos

39. Revival, Enlightenment, and Awakening – The Divine Intelligence of Eternity in Fire and Water

40. Eternity Volume 3 – The Ancient Realm, The Alpha Real, and the Realm Called Eden (TBR)

41. Divine Wisdom - The Lights of Wisdom in Wisdom (TBR)

42. Scientific Battles Against Humanity (TBR)

43. Beyond Earth (TBR)

44. Presences (TBR)

45. Authority and Power (TBR)

46. The Bodies of Man (TBR)

Available on amazon.com and its affiliates

Remarks on The Reality Series

Isn't it just so great when you find one of those books that completely drags you in, makes you fall in love with God and demands that you sit on the edge of your seat to discover the unknown? This (Book 19: Ecstasy: The Truth Concerning Pleasure and Happiness) is one of those books. Looking forward to reading it – more slowly and spending more time on the details of Pleasure.

Dinah Wanjiku

Reader in Nairobi Kenya

This book on oneness (book 16) is a heavenly Portal and not just a mere book like any other; it is. according to my language, a living epistle bearing the Spirit of the letter, that which quickens. You cannot be a Kingdom mystic in Christ and ignore this book. I am a living witness to what I have experienced and continue to experience Supernaturally through the Heavenly Portal of this book. I recommend that You Consider a Multi-dimensional journey of Supernatural experience by reading & analytically studying this book through the lens of the Spirit.

Apostle Joe Kennedy (Voice of Thunders)

Revival, Enlightenment, and Awakening   Joseph Kahuho Gatoto

House Of Thunders International

Mombasa, Kenya

I recommend this great curriculum to the Body of Christ all over the world, especially those who want to walk in the present-day manifestation of the sons of God. Every book is a sequence of the other. You cannot understand book 2 if you have not read book 1. I recommend if you are getting these books to get book 1.

Prophet Samuel Njagi

School of Supernatural Empowerment International

Kenya

This book (Book 7: Reality of Music) will stretch your understanding and implications of music in you as a becoming individual by helping you understand what music is, how music precedes man, and how every human has a propensity towards music.

Gift Isezerano

Reader in Nairobi, Kenya

Revival, Enlightenment, and Awakening   Joseph Kahuho Gatoto

I would recommend the book (7) to everyone who is musical and has been called to serve in the music ministry. It has deep insights unveiled to the world.

Mary Patricia Nyaboke

Librarian at Gospel Garden Bible School

Revival, Enlightenment, and Awakening   Joseph Kahuho Gatoto

Table of Contents

Dedication i

Introduction ii

Fire and Water... 1

Creation: The Mingling of Water and Fire 4

Introspection and Revival 8

Revival and Awakening 11

Asleep 13

We are All Asleep 16

Revival 19

Awakenings Within an Initial Awakening........................ 22

Consciousness, Revival, and Awakening 26

Heart Transformation... 29

Reviving the Earth 33

The Multiplicity of Revival 35

Dedication

To all seeking to grow and become more in the Everlasting

Spirit of Light and Love.

Introduction

As much as we speak of revival, we are yet to grasp its consummated reality. This is my cause in this work by divine grace.

In higher Divine terms of truth, revival is coming to the life of God and the knowledge thereof, which is God Himself. It, therefore, follows that revival comes with knowledge in knowledge and produces the same. The revived man is, thus, awakened and enlightened and progresses towards the same reality. Enlightenment and awakening are not a one-time affair. It is an eternal matter and reality with infinite subsequent realities. One cannot be revived and not awakened or enlightened in Eternity's reality of revival through and in His Alpha Reviving Vibration and Frequency, Himself. It is He that revives to Himself and in Himself bringing humanity to its original reality in Himself and from Himself. May you be revived in absolute and dimensional terms. May God wake us up from sleep. For, we are all asleep with some being more asleep than others.

Chapter 1

Fire and Water

"But the water that I shall give him will become in him a
fountain of water springing up into everlasting life." John
4:14 NKJV

In Divine symbolic terms, fire is the element of light and
water is the element of life (though these are one, God Who
is Eternal Light and Life). Water gives life; fire is the light
of life. And this life is Eternity. The fullness of life is fire
and water. Both Elements, Eternity - The One Infinite
Element, sustain and give life, to Himself. These are the
balance in His Structure, Himself. They are one rhythm, one
motion, an Eternal Constant State with no beginning and no
end being the Beginning and the End; and this is Himself.
And rightly, for water 'ends' fire, and fire heats and warms
the water. The same 'ends' water. Both change the state of
the other and manifest it in another state. Water turns fire to
smoke, which it produces in its burning, and fire turns and
manifests water as vapour. Each has power over the other.
Authority over the other to manifest the other in another
dimension of itself. And these manifestations are the glory
of each. Vapour is the glory of water; smoke is the glory of

fire. And not merely glories of, but glories in because they are produced from and have a different dimension of visibility; are a different dimension of the same element. There is a balanced effect of power and authority - balanced authority. Both cannot mingle and not change form. They change the form of each other. Being One Spirit, The Eternal Omnipotent Omniscient Spirit, these Divine Elements, One Element, The Divine Element; the change of form is the manifestation of the Divine Element's formless form. Both are without form. Fire has no form. Water has no form. They take forms per manipulation but do not have form. In the same way, the Eternal Spirit has no form. He is formless. And this is the Highest Perfect and Absolute Form, The Eternal Form, Which is the Divine Element. Consequently, you cannot change form, in Divine terms, to Divine Form and come to the Divine Form without fire and water. That is - without the light of His life and His life. One must come to the balance of harmony in Eternity, Himself, the constant motion of His Life, Himself, and the constant formations of Himself in Himself, His constant formations of His Formless Form in Himself, the constant mingling of fire and water that sustains Himself which is Himself. The Life of God in man is sustained by the constant mingling of fire and water with the proceeding manifestations of smoke and vapour, or moisture, which is termed as the Morning Dew, or the Dew of Heaven, Eternity Himself, and the consequent smoke as the darkness in which God dwells, which is Himself, the cloud of glory. God is Darkness! He dwells in Darkness and this is Himself. The Thick Clouds that Israel saw, the clouds of glory, are His life manifested. It is this that produces the glory of Eternity in man. Fire and water must forever mingle in the Christian.

Chapter 2

Creation: The Mingling of Water and Fire

"In the beginning God created the heavens and the earth."
Genesis 1:1 NKJV

Water changes the 'form' of fire and brings it to an 'end'. Fire changes the 'form' of water and brings it to an 'end'. The Cosmic Principle of Balanced Interchange, Harmony. Life and creation are because life mingles with Itself and mingled with Himself in Himself producing all kinds and sorts of forms, imaginings, which we and all of creation are. This mingling of fire and water is the interaction of Eternity in His male and female dimensions of Existence, which are Himself. The balanced mingling of God with Himself in Himself generated creation. The Balance of Eternity, in Eternity, Which is Eternity, is the base of all manifestation of all life forms. Consequently, all of creation exists in a state of balance. Balance is a Principle of Creation and, therefore, a Cosmic Principle of all beings in all the created realms of God. This is the Word, Christ from Whom and through Whom all things became and are. The Same sustains all things. Balance, the constant mingling of the Life of God with Himself, is what sustains all things. And this mingling, forever in interaction, is the flow and reflow of God in God, the static motion that is Eternity; the to and fro of Eternity in Eternity, the linear cyclic cycle of Eternity in Eternity. From whence Life comes, from Itself, there it goes and returns. The Linear Cyclic Cosmic Principle: "To the place from which the rivers come, There they return again." Ecclesiastes 1:7 (NKJV). The Principle is well portrayed from verses 5-10 of the same chapter. Creation follows where it came from. Eternity is the life-stream of creation. There is a constant mingling of creation and Eternity: from the beginning till now. For when He said let there be, Eternity was generating a life current, life vibration, creation, from Himself that will always depend on the flow from Himself. Creating was the act of generating a life-stream from the life-stream of Eternity, Himself. It follows that your life is an interaction with your life. Life, yourself is the flow of life from the self in the self from the One Life Stream. From this life happens to itself. You happen to yourself! What you do affects you. This applies with respect to the self-acting upon the self and the self-acting towards others. You reap what you sow. As the Life of Eternity flows in Eternity: from Eternity to Eternity eternally, so life flows from us to us in action and speech. Life is centrifugal and centripetal! life flows from life and to life. From yourself to yourself and from yourself to others and to yourself. This applies to the reality of life in its fullness (here, now, and in the hereafter). The same is justice. The mingling of fire and water and the effects thereof from the cause, the mingling, is justice. And this that mingles, the mingling is the Divine Element, Eternity, the Fire and the Water. The Mingling of Eternity with Eternity is the basis of all things. In Divine Symbolic terms, fire and water are the elements of justice in creation, are creation. All is fire and water in motion. And what is fire and water in motion if not the life-stream of Eternity, Himself. So, all things are manifestations of the Eternal Life Stream - The Flowing Essence of God, Himself under the guide and reality of the Cosmic Principle of Productivity that is Himself and is in Himself as the governance of His Reality, Himself, in His terms of existence, Himself. By the same Principle of Being and Existence, Himself, Revival, Awakening, and Enlightenment become and are! For these are for the realisation of the Principle of Productivity within and in the unity of the Cosmic Principles of Life, that are Life and the Governance therein. Consequently, humanity cannot be productive within Divine terms, and in the same, without Revival, Awakening and Enlightenment. They are necessities of productivity in the parameters of Eternity. Productivity is through becoming. You produce as you become and produce to become. Becoming and Productivity are inseparable. The principles are inseparable.

Volume 1

Introspection and Revival

"You shall love your neighbour as yourself." Mark 12:31 NKJV

Creation, as noted earlier, is a manifestation of self-integration, self-mingling, Eternity mingling with Himself in Himself. The same is a platform of Divine Manifestation and Productivity. It is impossible to be productive without self-interaction in both self and divine terms. And since Revival is coming to the Life of God, Himself, and the life we are in Him, which produced all things, yourself included, from the platform of self-interaction, Revival is inseparable from the reality of introspection. Introspection is a divine tendency and attribute. It is practising the Divine Mind and Nature. Consequently, the man growing in Divinity and coming to their divine nature interacts with himself. In truth, a healthy self-relationship, and a growing one for that matter, is a sign of a higher soul on the grand scale of souls. Your association determines your elevation and ascension in life. Verily, the same determines, in certain terms of Eternity and in Eternity, your relationship with Him and in Him. This encompasses engaging the Elevating, and Awakening Alpha Vibrations of

Eternity. For, the man that sees into himself and knows himself better is elevated and awakened. You are a channel of self-awakening and elevation. Self-relationship provokes the Awakening and Elevating Alpha Vibrations of Eternity causing Enlightenment. An introspective man is enlightened, the eyes of their understanding are with light. The man that sees into himself sees better. It follows that Revival enhances self-perception, self-understanding, and self-awareness. It is the desire of Eternity that we associate with ourselves and grow in the knowledge of ourselves in self-creating terms and divine terms. Ergo, Revival has much to do with self-relationships. A revived man is brought to self-relationship (self-love), and self-awareness. It follows that self-relationship is a dimension of revival and working of the Alpha Vibrations of Eternity in humanity. Truly, when we come to Him, He brings us to ourselves in the initial awakening when we are Revived in Him through Christ. To be revived is to be brought to the self. The self and its association with Itself is of paramount significance and import to Eternity. This is seen in scripture multiple times. From the Beginning, Himself, when God made Adam in His Image and Likeness, from a dimension, His Humanity, of Himself from Himself by Himself. You are part of the Beginning and to This, you are brought back through

Revival to become the same through the Cosmic Linear Cyclic Principle that you also are. From where you came there you return. Revival returns you to yourself in Him from Whom you came to become.

Chapter 3

Revival and Awakening

"Consider and hear me, O LORD my God;

Enlighten my eyes,

Lest I sleep the sleep of death..." Psalm 13:3 NKJV

The awakened are enlightened. These are with fire, they are fire. They see in the Light; they see from the Light seeing as the Light and grow in seeing as the Light sees thereby knowing as the Light knows in learning to know as He knows. They are the Light of the Cosmos! The awakened are not asleep! They are awake and watch. For this reason, it is the fire that awakens. The Omnipotent Spirit enlightens. He is the Spirit of Enlightenment. The Light through which, from which, and in which the mind understands the Divine. Unless you are awakened you cannot know as you should know. Forms are not known in the dark but in the light. Unless there is light, one cannot read; one cannot understand. There is no understanding in darkness. Only in the Light. Consequently, you cannot know you as you should unless you are enlightened by the Enlightening Spirit. For the you that you know as you, your present self, is a dimension of the Infinite and Eternal Spirit, Eternity, Whose

Light is Forever Illuminated and Illuminating. All things are known as they are by the Enlightening Spirit. Those in the dark don't see those in the Light. But those in the Light see those in the darkness. And so, those in the Light reach those in the darkness by sharing the Light of the Ages, Eternity! The Everlasting Gospel of Truth that is Christ Jesus. Anyone in Christ is in the Light; is the Light, Who is the Awakened and Enlightened One walking in the Light as the Light and is the Light.

Chapter 4

Asleep

"How long will you slumber, O sluggard?

When will you rise from your sleep?" Proverbs 6:9 NKJV

Now, if you are awakened, it is because you were asleep. The sleeping ones are not conscious of the realm of the living, in certain terms, though they are living. The man that is asleep doesn't know what the man that is awake is doing. The awakened sees the sleeping man but the sleeping man doesn't see nor know the awakened. So then, what is meant by asleep is lack of a certain state of consciousness within a state of consciousness. The sleeping man is living, is conscious and so is the awakened man. There is, however, a difference in dimensions of existence and awareness. The man sleeping is aware of the dimension of dreams and the man that was once asleep is aware of the dimension of dreams, though he is not asleep, and of the awakened. Let it be understood that these two are in the same realm but in two different states of living, dimensions of life. To be asleep is to lack the necessary knowledge for living: certain elementary truths or otherwise. In biblical, cum Christian terms, the sleeping man is a child in need of milk. Milk

13

enlightens toward meat. That is - elementary truths, doctrines, build capacity to chew higher truths, doctrines of the Higher Realms and beyond to the Highest Civilization and Realm, Eternity. Along the same path, it is those that are awake that eat. The sleeping man doesn't eat. As a matter of truth, the sleeping man cannot eat nor be fed. He must be woken up and then fed. In their sleep, the sleeping must be roused by a longing for something greater than life, than the concerns of their physical reality. A hunger beyond what to eat, and drink in providence or absence of both. And from that hunger, a cry: "What must we do to be saved?!" That is - what must we do to be awakened. Which is: what must we do to be brought up to the reality and realities of Christ, the Awakened, Enlightened, and Enlightening Eternal Spirit. This is the goal of being awakened within the reality of Christ. Many in Him are asleep, many believers, Christians have fallen asleep in His company and these have failed to watch. A sleeping man doesn't watch. Those awake watch and pray. Consequently, the praying man is a watching man. One that has been awakened and is being awakened in their awakening in Christ. These are in the Light, fire, are with fire; and have not fallen asleep in the Light. The same are those that have let their light shine. It is those in the wake state that light fires and keep the Light on! May we not sleep in the Light but wake to the Light and become like the Light.

Volume 1

We are All Asleep

"And *do* this, knowing the time, that now *it is* high time to awake out of sleep; for now our salvation *is* nearer than when we *first* believed." Romans 13:11 NKJV

We are conscious but not fully conscious of our conscious activities. We are all conscious but not fully conscious of our consciousness, of ourselves. Thus, we are asleep though awake. Thus, we are awake in dimensional terms in our waking state for we are not fully conscious of ourselves in the same reality of wakeness. You don't know you though you know you. To be awakened conjoins the reality of self-awakening. Be awakened to the self, in self terms. We are to be brought to the reality of ourselves, of the consciousness we are. This involves the faculty of memory, an awareness of all that resides therein in real-time, in the now. The Now is real-time. This is knowing all you know in the now. For you know many things but do not know that you know them. Further, it involves being conscious of our conscious activities in our sleep state: of the portion of you that sleeps and the portion of you that does not sleep and the yous from the you that does not sleep. To, therefore, awaken means to come to the reality of our consciousness and to be aware of our multiple locational reality in self-expansion terms: in self from self-generating terms and the activities of these. The same includes being conscious of the action of sleeping. You can be conscious that you are sleeping because sleep is a manifestation of consciousness. It is consciousness manifesting and to be conscious is to be conscious of consciousness in the reality of its multiplicity. This is a dimension of high consciousness and of higher vibratory frequential dimensional realities in Eternity conjoined to self-knowledge. Self-knowledge is being conscious of consciousness and its multiplicity of knowing and manifestation within and in its multiplicity, which is itself. To be awakened is to be conscious of consciousness that is to be conscious of the self in and within its divine nature and reality with the manifestations therein. This is the future of self-knowledge and self-awareness. Consequently, we are all asleep though awake. We are in a state of semi-consciousness in our wake state with sleep being a semi-consciousness state within a semi-conscious state. There are, however, men that live in expanded consciousness. That is - in a higher awakened state of consciousness where they are highly conscious in their sleep and highly conscious in their wake state conjoined to heighten and increased self-consciousness and awareness. There are others higher than these, and these are fully aware of themselves in dimensional and becoming terms and are in a higher dimension of Known and Unknown (the Cosmic Principle). Everyone knows and doesn't know. You know you but don't know you. Even these, higher in the Known and Unknown Cosmic Reality, know themselves and do not know themselves. The selves that they are, themselves, are always manifesting from themselves as they become. They are ever in a becoming state of higher consciousness (self-awareness and self-knowledge). This is our reality of being and becoming. We are all asleep with some more being asleep than others. We are all awake but some are more awake than others. May we wake up and be woken up. May we awaken.

Chapter 5

Revival

"And to the angel of the church in Sardis write,
'These things says He who has the seven Spirits of God and
the seven stars: "I know your works, that you have a name
that you are alive, but you are dead." Revelation 3:1 NKJV

It is the awakened that revive! Unless you are awake you
cannot revive anything. Revival comes from the Enlightened
Ones. These are channels, and pathways, of fire and light.
The push and wake-up call that sleepers and the dead need.
Notice: sleepers and the dead. In certain spiritual terms, a
sleeping man is a dead man, in dimensional terms, though he
lives. If he sleeps for long, he dies. In Christian lingo, this is
called backsliding. Existing outside the parameters of
Eternity in utter darkness. It takes God to wake these up.
Now, it is very much possible to seem awake but you are
asleep and or dead. You can have a reputation of being alive,
yet you are dead in dimensional and total terms to both men
and yourself. This happens when one retains an appearance
of Christ, or spirituality, but lacks the vitality and power, the
life force that is Christ. Seeming as Christ but not Christ.
Such are caught up in spiritual activities, church activities,

19

and giving but are not participants of Christ, some were but are not anymore. It's a slow fade that takes discernment and sensitivity to know. As stated by Casting Crowns: "People never crumble in a day." Falls don't happen instantly but progressively. One doesn't regress in the grand scale of souls in a day. It takes time. It's a process. Regression is progressive.

The dimensional terms of death related to the reality of the multiplicity of humanity, the multiplicity that is you, within the parameters of Eternity and the administrations of that Life has diverse causes: People can get hurt and stop serving, giving, and helping the needy. The same can be as a result of being manipulated and deceived. There is always a cause for death (in absolute and dimensional terms). With others it's losing hope, losing faith, betrayal in the Church, being hurt by spiritual authorities, pain from believers and etcetera. All these cause death in dimensional and absolute terms. Death in dimensional terms means that there is a dimension of an individual that lacks the Life of Eternity. A dimension of being lacking the expression of the Life of Eternity. That is - is not permeated by Eternity and functions under the confines of the flesh, the sinful nature, that is contrary to Eternity. As it is often stated: twice beaten, twice shy.

Among other causes is a lack of a listening ear, a discerning ear, and intelligence in giving. We are told to give but not without discernment. Not every ground is for sowing. Not every need is genuine, and not every beggar is genuine. Beyond the mentioned, one may be walking right but struggling with certain dark tendencies such as lying, sexual immorality, and failure to trust God when it comes to relationships. Any area you don't trust God in is an area housing death and needs life, a revival. Consequently, revival entails oneness with Eternity. A bringing of humanity to its godhood in Eternity. Godhood is attained through a revival in dimensional terms to the awakened ones. This is because an awakened one or a sleeping one may be dead in dimensional terms. Gods are fully awakened; they are not asleep in any reality of their being. These do not know sleep or death in dimensional terms. Some were asleep, dead, and dead in dimensional terms but they were awakened, and enlightened towards becoming the Awakened and Enlightened Ones.

Chapter 6

Awakenings Within an Initial Awakening

"...the eyes of your understanding being enlightened; that you may know what is the hope of His calling, what are the riches of the glory of His inheritance in the saints..."

Ephesians 1:8 NKJV

In truth, Revival and Awakening set men towards the path of self consummation, towards higher dimensions of themselves that ultimately consummate in the Higher Self over a continuous infinite process of becoming, of awakenings within the initial awakening - of enlightenments within the initial enlightenment. You must be an initiate through awakening to come to the awakenings in awakening. Consequently, awakening and revival are inseparable from the becoming process of humanity and the awakening of the potential and potencies of humanity to its reality in Eternity, Who is Humanity. It is a matter of nature, the unveiling and restoration of human nature to humanity, It's godhood and operation as gods in Eternal terms of being beyond human parameters of its own definition. There is humanity in human terms and humanity in Eternal terms. Most dwell on the former and have accepted the definition taking in the limitations ascribed by the same. Humanity is beyond flesh and blood; the reality of man is not in man in certain terms but in Eternity in absolute terms. Not in humanity because what every man is, Eternity is and the Same is the origin of what every man is. Before every man was, The One and Every Man was, which is Eternity. The One New Man is The One and Every Man! The Awakened and Enlightened One Which is Christ, Who is Eternity. Christ is the Prime Man, Prime Humanity. He is humanity manifested in the reality of revival and awakening. That is - after being revived and awakened in being revived, humanity matures toward Christ. It is not merely about a demonstration of power but manifestation and manifestations of nature, the nature of the Eternal Spirit in humanity, and humanity in the reality of humanity in the Eternal Spirit, which is Christianity. It follows that what transpires in the reality of revival and awakening (with its subsequent awakenings) is, in dimensional terms of Eternity's Humanity, the revelation of humanity per the terms of Eternity. It is ascribed, and was ascribed, by Eternity via His Divine Prerogative in the Prerogative Court, Himself, that humanity operates in the Divine Nature being eternal in nature (what revival and awakening are all about). Humanity is Eternity and the workings of Eternity in humanity are within the parameters of what humanity is in Eternal terms as demonstrated and revealed by Christ. Wasn't the revival in the book of Acts a result of Eternity in humanity? Was it not the Eternal Spirit manifesting through men within the parameters of Eternity? Was it not humanity operating in one of the realities of their Prime State in Prime Reality, Who is The Prime State of Being and is ever in the Prime State of Being? It is when humanity is in Eternity, and progressively growing in the Same, that humanity functions as humanity (per the Absolute immutable Verdict of the Eternal Prerogative Court and Government, Eternity)! As it is written: "Let us make man in our image and likeness..." Genesis 1:26 NKJV. This is an absolute, immutable, irrevocable and irreversible verdict. The same is, let us make man to be a participant and reality of our nature in and through becoming terms. Eternity is the Purpose of humanity. The same is attained through the channel of destiny, which is from Purpose, Eternity. Destiny is not an end in itself but a pointer to a greater reality, a greater end, Purpose (Eternity). To earn more on Purpose and Destiny read Becoming Divine - The Destiny of Humanity in the same series). So then, the initial awakening is to nature, human nature and Eternity in Whom the nature is concealed, and the subsequent awakenings are to the realities of the natures, the natures within the nature to the for the perfection of the nature, that is for humanity to become Consummate and Consummated, an absolute infinite process. Revival ends! But awakening doesn't end. To be revived is to come to a greater reality, awakening and the subsequent(s) of the same in the parameters of revival. Remember: it is the awakened that Revive because they have been revived and have become awakened and are in the reality and progressive reality of awakening to its consummate end - maturing in the Eternal Nature: "...to the full stature of Christ."

Chapter 7

Consciousness, Revival, and Awakening

"And the LORD God formed man of the dust of the ground, and breathed into his nostrils the breath of life, and man became a living being." Genesis 2:7 NKJV

To be is to have consciousness. Humanity is, therefore, consciousness and is conscious. To know is to grow in consciousness through understanding, will, emotions, and memory. To be conscious of something is to be able to remember it having known it through understanding, will, and the faculties of the mind. You remember what you have known through understanding. Memory is a sign of consciousness. The same is not attached to forgetfulness in Eternal terms but the present state of knowing, where all things are known in the now and are present in the now. Memory is a dimension of consciousness. It follows that revival and awakening have an effect on and affect consciousness. You cannot be revived and not be brought to a higher vibratory frequential dimensional reality of consciousness. The same applies to being awakened and to the subsequent awakenings. As stated elsewhere in the read, you are revived to your nature, brought to the life you are in Eternity. This is conjoined to a reality of consciousness. The dead are revived, brought to a reality of consciousness relating to their existence. When you are revived it is to your nature in Eternity, the nature of Eternity. This is your ordained lot in Eternity. Your inheritance is beyond the physical realm. The same comes with the vitality and power of nature. So, the revived man is brought into the reality of the power of Eternity; not to merely be a witness but to operate in it being in the same power, the One Eternal Power, Eternity. The reviving of nature is coming to the power of the nature. Note: a witness of power is not necessarily the wielder of the power. But in Eternal terms, we are to be wielder and witnesses of His Power, Himself. There are some, however, that are stationed to be witnesses due to their hardened hearts. Now, the same power that revives and works in the revived, gives consciousness, gave consciousness, and elevates consciousness. The elevation of consciousness is awakenings within the initial awakening. The ascension of humanity is inseparable from subsequent awakenings. A working of the Elevating Alpha Frequency and Vibrations preceded by the operations of the Reviving Alpha Frequency and Vibrations of Eternity. The same vibrations are the Eternal Frequency expressed and operating within Its Infinite and Unsearchable Multiplicity. Consequently, Revival and Awakening are the operations of the Eternal Frequency. Radiations of the Eternal Light in and through its Vibration and Frequency. Additionally, it means that revival and awakening (with the subsequent awakenings) are frequency modulation. The raising of frequencies and vibrations to the Highest and Most Elevated One - Eternity. Revival and Awakening alter the state of your vibration and heart. These are Frequency Modulations.

Chapter 8

Heart Transformation

"And do not be conformed to this world, but be transformed by the renewing of your mind, that you may prove what is that good and acceptable and perfect will of God." Romans 12:2 NKJV

Your heart cannot remain the same when you are revived. The same cannot remain the same when you are awakened. It is the inner dimensions of your constitution that are changed for you to be revived and awakened. Water cleans the heart, and makes it pure and clean. Fire destroys the impurities making it clean. Fire and Water change the heart. These two are in a mingling state. In oneness. That is - the association of Eternity with Himself in Eternity and the mingling of humanity with Eternity for the mingling of humanity with itself in itself. Fire and Water, Eternity's mingling with Himself, generates the mingling of man with his inner realities for the mingling of man with fellow man. Self-association is the platform of person-to-person association. The heart must, therefore, be transformed in relation to itself. Revival and awakening change self-relationship, create self-awareness and advance self-awareness. The revived are brought to self-consciousness: "...and the man became a living being..." That is - and the man became self-aware. Self-awareness is a sign and reality of revival and awakening. And what is self-awareness? Is it not Self Enlightenment, awakening to the self, knowing the self. The Spirit transforms the heart and creates self-awareness. In certain terms, self-awareness is the mark of an enlightened soul, a revived soul. An agent of revival. A transformer heart is a revived heart, an awakened awakening heart. The same is tender, soft, and contrite. A contrite heart is self-knowing! And these the Lord will not reject. Verily, a revived and awakened man is like a child but is not a child. The revived are made children to become sons in their variegated dimensions through awakenings in the initial awakening by revival. And these, awakenings, come from a heart that is like a child's heart. This is innocence. Revival and Awakening is the restoration of innocence. Restoring humanity to innocence. It is this that is meant by being as a child but not being a child. Purity is by innocence, wisdom, knowledge, understanding, honour, and the realities of love are innocence. A pure heart is an innocent heart. Purity is innocence. Humanity in Eternal terms is in a state of innocence. Eternity is Innocence. Love is Innocence. To love Someone is to be like a child (with them) but not to be a child. Submission is to be as a child but to be a child. To love is to be as a child but not be a child! Submission is innocence. It follows that heart transformation is towards the reality and realities of innocence. Where one knows and knows that they do not know even if they know. For in their knowing they know that what they know is greater than what they do not know: that what they know is a drop in the ocean (Socrates). Again, this is walking in love, the nature of humanity, of Eternity, which is kind, selfless, patient, honourable, pure, honest, authentic, and all potent. Innocence is All-Powerful. It is in innocence that we know the Power of God and minister in the same, and know as we ought to know. May we be given innocent hearts. Again, to walk in purity is to walk in innocence. The pure is innocent. The innocent is highly enlightened, highly potent, wise, knowing, and great in understanding. It is only an innocent mind that can earn the Eternal Spirit and operate from the same. Therefore, when it is said that we are partakers of the Eternal Nature, it is that we are partakers of the innocence of Eternity. The Nature of Innocence. Innocence is an Eternal Nature. A state of Being! A dimensional Reality of Eternity, it is the Immutable Reality of Eternity. Eternity is Innocence. The Holy Spirit is Innocence. This innocence is humanity's ordained and true nature. It is one who is as a child but is not a child that is the Absolute Potency of Eternity, this is Eternity. Fire and Water are innocent agents of innocence. In fire and water dwells the intelligence of innocence. Consequently, a transformed heart is brought to Eternal Understanding, Knowledge, Wisdom, and Peace. Again, the most elevated souls are in a state of innocence.

Chapter 9

Reviving the Earth

"For we know that the whole creation groans and labours with birth pangs together until now." Romans 8:22 NKJV

As goes the man, so goes the earth. Whatever man becomes the Earth becomes. Humanity is the architect of the Earth. When humanity is restored to its original state, so is the Earth. Man's revival revives the Earth, man's awakening transforms the Earth. Self Awareness transforms the Earth. The man that is self-aware in the confines of Eternity, radiates the vibrations of love that mutate the Earth and Cosmos to the vibration and reality of Love, Eternity. To walk in Love is to radiate the potencies of Love to the whole of creation. Now, creation awaits the manifestation of sons. Sons are born by being revived and grow through subsequent awakenings. The Earth and physical cosmos await the manifestation of the awakened and awakening sons in their variant degrees of ranking. Some are asleep and others dead in dimensional and absolute terms, and when these are awakened and revived in dimensional and absolute terms, the Earth and the Cosmos will be restored to its fruitfulness. Futility will be taken away from it. That is - when humanity is in a state of purity, Innocence, the Earth will be restored to its original state. Innocence redeems the Earth and Cosmos. Fire and Water are the intelligence of redemption in absolute terms of reality. Innocence is the potency of Earth and Cosmos Recreation! The same is the nature of gods in their variegated dimensions of existence and being. The Awakened and Enlightened Ones awaken the nature of things. The hidden original state and or realities of what is seen. There is what you see and know and there is what you don't see and know about what you see and know. The former is the present reality, the latter the original state before the fall (this is unknown). And yet, this is the workmanship of man's architectural design within the parameters of Eternity in its original state, like the humanity that Eternity is. Revival is appointed to manifest the glory of the Earth and the Cosmos to take away the dress and blanket of futility to which Earth was subjected in hope.

Chapter 10

The Multiplicity of Revival

"...even when we were dead in trespasses, made us alive

together with Christ (by grace you have been saved) ..."

Ephesians 2:5 NKJV

Revival is coming to the life of God from death (in dimensional and absolute terms). The life of God, Himself, is Unsearchable and Deeply Mysterious and Mystical carrying and containing Mystical and Mysterious Powers within His Absolute Power, Himself; Who is His Sceptre of Authority and Power. The Same is Infinite in multiplicity, is Infinite Multiplicity. Consequently, a coming to His Life is coming to the reality of His Multiplicity, to Infinite Multiplicity wherein humanity has been appointed and is appointed by Divine Prerogative to reside and manifest from, coming to Eternity having come to Eternity ad infinitum. And so, in the past ages revival through the Alpha Reviving Frequency and Vibrations in certain dimensions of the Same per the ordained and willed manifestation of Eternity in the respective times, dispensations, within time for the gathering of all things to Himself has manifested and carried aspects of His Life, Himself. These revivals have

35

carried manifestations of the Life of Eternity but were not and are not the fullness of this Life. Revival has infinite dimensions, the Alpha Reviving Frequency and Vibration has infinite operations within the parameters of Eternity for bringing humanity to Its reality and life in Eternity, Who is Humanity in absolute terms. Eternity is the One and Every Man that is all and every man in their prime. Each is a fragment of Him in His Humanity, Himself, beyond physical terms and in physical terms. And to this, the reality of The One and Every Man, the One New Man, Christ, does Eternity work in revival to being all men to Himself and to themselves in Himself. That is - to the infinite multiplicity of themselves in Himself. This entails creativity, and innovation in technological and architectural design - restoring man to their godhood and the creations and innovations that are primary to the exercise of their dominion dovetailed to intelligence, understanding, intelligence, knowledge, and wisdom - the reality of the Seven Spirits, Expansions of Eternity. Furthermore, there are dimensions of the same that relate to bringing man to mystical and mysterious operations within their multiplicities such as self-expansion conjoined to being in multiple places at the same time, being able to travel in between the realms, teleportation, telepathy, and visions, and all such realities that relate to the life of Eternity and of humanity in Eternity. For this reason, the previous revivals have had such manifestations that included the reviving of the body - bringing it to its original intended design and form through healing. Revival restores all things and brings all things to their original intended design and the realities therein that encapsulate functions within the parameters of the life of Eternity. Verily, revival affects the whole of man and takes Him into His reality of being in Divine terms. It is man coming to His operations with God, where we operate like God in God in oneness with the Same. This takes men on a journey in themselves to their Higher Selves, dimensions of Eternity that are Eternity, to become as He is. Revival restores men to Purpose through Destiny. For this reason, men in times past have been brought to destiny by being brought to Purpose, where they reside in Self Awareness and Knowledge as Eternity is. Revival brings men to self-knowledge in present and future terms in light of Christ - the Now and Future Man in every dimension of humanity - intelligence, body, memory, understanding, knowledge, authority, wisdom, multi-locus existence, kindness, mercy, ecstasy, strength, honour, selflessness, patience and as many as are the infinite natures of Eternity wherein there is neither male nor female but humanity and

Eternity is All in All and becoming All in All in all that is humanity. For the humanity in Eternity is full of Eternity! It is nothing but Eternity in substance and essence and this is what we are to become in revival and ascend to through revival in our present becoming in our infinite becoming process that is ourselves. You are the journey of your life. Consequently, revival is an ascension. The revived have ascended to ascend in ascending to higher frequential vibratory dimensional realities in Eternity, to higher versions of themselves in their Highest Infinite and Eternal Version, Eternity, in dimensional within dimensional terms, in His Humanity dimension, Himself. So then, we are revived to manifest as God in our godhood and to operate within the parameters of God. That is - in our divinity and potency in Eternity which is to operate as gods in God commanding nature and the elements with mutating the same for divine manifestations of healing and restoration of humanity to Eternity and the functionaries therein.